RISE

AN AUTHENTIC LENTEN DEVOTIONAL

JOHN PAVLOVITZ

chalice
press

Saint Louis, Missouri

An imprint of Christian Board of Publication

ChalicePress.com

Print: 9780827233119
EPUB: 9780827233126   EPDF: 9780827233133

Printed in the United States of America

Introduction

I was recently watching the movie *Batman Begins* (for roughly the 83rd time). One of my favorite scenes shows a battered Bruce Wayne surrounded by the burning rubble of the family estate he inherited after his parents' deaths. He is the keeper of their legacy, the steward of the family name, the carrier of their memory—and he feels as though he has failed to do all of these things. His longtime butler and father-figure, Alfred, repeats words to Bruce that Bruce's father often shared with him as a child, in moments of discouragement in order to steady him.

He says, "Why do we fall, Bruce?"

Bruce's father's reply still echoes in his head: "So we can get back up."

This is a wonderful moment in the film, but I'm not sure it's great theology: the idea that pain has a purpose. I don't believe our suffering is a premeditated test that forces us to find meaning, but I believe that pain is a present opportunity to choose: a sacred space where we get to decide who we will be and what we will believe and how we will respond. As people of faith, we get up when we fall because we are a people of hope, we accept the descent as the invitation to rise again. The spiritual journey—like the human experience—is not a level, linear path where pitfalls are uniform and where growth is predictable and progress comfortable. It is a messy, meandering, awkward path of stops and starts. It is made of both the falling and the getting back up—and the former is often far easier than the latter.

Rising is inherent in our religious tradition:
We allow our spirits to rise in the middle of the storms.
We wait for the sun to rise, trusting that a joyful morning will follow a night of mourning.

We rise to our feet after falling to our knees in desperate prayer, assured that we are not alone in the struggle.

We rise in resilience when person and circumstance knock the wind from us.

We rise to meet the coming day, knowing we are held by a Love that endures through the blackest darkness.

We rise on the promise that death is not that final word.

Lent is not an event. It's not just one, glorious moment. As much as being about a single dawn arriving, it is about all the many not-yets, one-day-soons, and still-to-comes of this life in the waiting, about the painful in-between times that we'd like to fast-forward through on our way to peace and growth and clarity. That seems to be where the bulk of the rising happens. Maybe that's a good way to think of our time together here in these pages: in the valley places but with our eyes still looking up.

This is a season ultimately made of elevated hopes, raised expectations, ascending spirits, and radiant mornings, and we should never forget that. It is love helping us get back up. But before all of that, it is a road that travels through the darkness, through the waiting, through grief, and through the nights where hope feels beyond reach. Those are sacred spaces too, even if they are less pleasant. Consider these pages a journey *to* something and a journey *through* something. As keepers of a legacy and stewards of a family name and carriers of a memory, we can be encouraged that when we are presently falling, the rise is never far away.

1) The Windshield and the Rearview Mirror

After the sabbath, at dawn on the first day of the week, Mary Magdalene and the other Mary went to look at the tomb.

There was a violent earthquake, for an angel of the Lord came down from heaven and, going to the tomb, rolled back the stone and sat on it. His appearance was like lightning, and his clothes were white as snow. The guards were so afraid of him that they shook and became like dead men.

The angel said to the women, "Do not be afraid, for I know that you are looking for Jesus, who was crucified. He is not here; he has risen, just as he said. Come and see the place where he lay. Then go quickly and tell his disciples, 'He has risen from the dead and is going ahead of you into Galilee. There you will see him.' Now I have told you."

So the women hurried away from the tomb, afraid yet filled with joy, and ran to tell his disciples. Suddenly Jesus met them. "Greetings," he said. They came to him, clasped his feet and worshiped him. Then Jesus said to them, "Do not be afraid. Go and tell my brothers to go to Galilee; there they will see me."

—MATTHEW 28:1–10

Spoiler alert: the tomb was empty. (I hope you don't stop reading now.)

It might seem strange to begin this journey with the end of the story (or at least with the culmination of the Lenten narrative), but I think it's helpful in framing every moment of the coming season for us. Starting in sunlit, tomb-side morning euphoria reminds us that the assurance of the dawn's arrival isn't easily claimed in the lightless moments. In fact, it's something that we often imagine will never come. When our struggles are in the windshield, when they are part of our present discomfort, it's nearly impossible to remember that they will one day be in our rearview mirror: that in one way or another we will have passed through something and reached something else, and that it will yield a stronger, wiser, more perceptive version of ourselves. We can't fathom now that we will eventually experience stratospheric joy despite the depth of the despair preceding it, but that is the greater story.

When we step into these forty days as people of faith, we do so while having the end in mind, and so the pain we encounter in the gospels is always tempered by the knowledge of the glorious morning we know is coming. It will be a path woven through doubt, grief, fear, and hopelessness, but we know how it ends, and that helps. We understand that the journey to the empty tomb always passes through the desperate garden prayers, through the brutal chaos of the cross, and through the absolute certainty that all is indeed lost—but that is never the last word.

I imagine this declaration isn't so easy regarding the current burdens you carry and the battles you wage right in this moment. Today, take solace in remembering that this isn't the end of the story, that it may simply be the struggle in the windshield. Soon it will be in the rear view.

2) A Holy Unavailability

Very early in the morning, while it was still dark, Jesus got up, left the house and went off to a solitary place, where he prayed. Simon and his companions

went to look for him, and when they found him,
they exclaimed: "Everyone is looking for you!"

Jesus replied, "Let us go somewhere else—to the
nearby villages—so I can preach there also. That
is why I have come." So he traveled throughout
Galilee, preaching in their synagogues and driving
out demons.

—MARK 1:35–39

"What was better when you were younger?"

Today, I posed that question on social media. The answers were a mix of lighthearted childhood touchstones such as sugary breakfast cereals and Saturday morning cartoons, personal mid-life lamentations about expanding waistlines and receding hairlines, and more somber observations about our public discourse and general level of empathy.

One of the things I think we were all better at in the past was *presence*. Before cell phones and prior to being perpetually available to everyone, when we were at the movies or at a concert or with our friends or walking in nature, we were fully there without interruption or dilution. We weren't continually being pulled to other places or alerted to more supposedly pressing matters or distracted with capturing our private moments for public consumption. This inability to be present comes from the fact that we are almost never truly alone or able to find protracted moments of complete solitude. Being unavailable is a lost art, one we would be wise to recover.

I love the moments in the gospels where Jesus withdraws to the silence and the stillness because they remind me that doing so isn't a betrayal of our work or the people in our path, but a way of preparing us to be fully present to it all. In those times when we pull away from the crowd (if we can), our minds are recalibrated and our reserves replenished; and when we return to the world, we are better able to offer our undivided selves. So, yes, the technology will always be a challenge, but the real and enduring danger is our own preoccupation with being reachable and the fear that we will miss out on something if we are not. If you want to be better at presence, work on absence first. Today, may you give yourself the gift of disappearing. May you do the sacred work of being unavailable.

3) The Wall of Resentment

"Therefore, if you are offering your gift at the altar and there remember that your brother or sister has something against you, leave your gift there in front of the altar. First go and be reconciled to them; then come and offer your gift."

—MATTHEW 5:23–24

I was preparing to speak at a Boise church and started having a conversation with a couple in the front row about the relational fractures of the recent days and the toll it was taking on them. One of the women commented on how upside down things seemed and how frustrated she was with people she knows and loves, and she said with sarcasm, "John, I'm 59 years old and I've been suicidal many times, but until recently I've never been homicidal." She laughed explosively afterward, realizing the darkness of the statement especially given the setting—but I knew what she meant. We've all been surprised by our vengeful hearts, and we know the wall anger makes between ourselves and others.

Grief, and even anger, are natural biproducts of being a person of empathy witnessing the cruelty in the world, but they can become a toxic cocktail and lead to something really unhealthy and unhelpful: resentment. This is that step beyond the natural mourning or reasonable outrage and into something worrisome, something punitive. Our resentment often comes from a desire to make someone "pay": for their vote, their politics, their theology, their hateful words, their corrosive beliefs. We want people to be held accountable—whatever that looks like to us. And along with that, we often would like for them to feel remorse or sorrow. We want people to confess, to show contrition, to express regret, or at least to admit they've done something wrong. But the problem is, these are often things they aren't able or willing to give us, at least right now. This unwillingness or inability is our invitation to decide what we will do in response. The issue with resentment isn't whether or not we agree with someone. That's almost irrelevant. The questions for people of faith, morality, and conscience are, how do I express disagreement, and what happens in my heart toward those I disagree with?

Today, consider the things you hold over or hold against someone, and how these might be holding you back from experiencing the fullness of the present.

4) A Nagging Pain

Just then a woman who had been subject to bleeding for twelve years came up behind him and touched the edge of his cloak. She said to herself, "If I only touch his cloak, I will be healed."

Jesus turned and saw her. "Take heart, daughter," he said, "your faith has healed you." And the woman was healed at that moment.

—MATTHEW 9:20–22

Not long ago I found myself at the doctor's office after experiencing some prolonged lower back discomfort. The physician examining me asked a question that you've likely been asked by a medical professional at some point: "One a scale of one to ten, how much pain are you experiencing right now?" I managed a half-smile and said, "Well, I'm hoping this is actually a nine, but it could turn out to only be a three. I'm afraid that things could get a lot more painful than they are right now." The doctor laughed but I wasn't kidding. I'd had enough irritation to bring me into that office, and I was really hoping that feeling worse was not a strong possibility. It wasn't just the severity of the pain but the duration that had worn me out.

We can get spoiled reading the healing stories in the gospels because they seem so instantaneous and complete: Jesus encounters someone with an affliction, and in a moment they are given total relief. They proceed to leave the story, seemingly no longer burdened by their afflictions and never to be heard from again. But in reality, healing is rarely so cut-and-dried, and that can be frustrating. Our suffering lingers; our recovery is sporadic; our progress faces setbacks—and sometimes we get worse.

I'm grateful that the gospel writer tells us of the dozen years prior to the bleeding woman's meeting Jesus, because we can understand her frustration and find ourselves in her story of chronic sickness or struggle. The greater challenge is in reading of her sudden reversal and not getting impatient. We want that dramatic and decisive kind of relief, and yet that isn't usually how the road to the rise happens. This season, you may be carrying a physical illness, an emotional burden, or a spiritual ailment that seems to be in no hurry to depart, and you may be in the early part of the journey and not necessarily near the end. Be encouraged. This doesn't mean you won't eventually find relief—it just may mean this day will be part of the waiting.

5) Love Remains

"I am the true vine, and my Father is the gardener. He cuts off every branch in me that bears no fruit, while every branch that does bear fruit he prunes so that it will be even more fruitful. You are already clean because of the word I have spoken to you. Remain in me, as I also remain in you. No branch can bear fruit by itself; it must remain in the vine. Neither can you bear fruit unless you remain in me.

"I am the vine; you are the branches. If you remain in me and I in you, you will bear much fruit; apart from me you can do nothing. If you do not remain in me, you are like a branch that is thrown away and withers; such branches are picked up, thrown into the fire and burned. If you remain in me and my words remain in you, ask whatever you wish, and it will be done for you. This is to my Father's glory, that you bear much fruit, showing yourselves to be my disciples.

"As the Father has loved me, so have I loved you. Now remain in my love. If you keep my commands, you will remain in my love, just as I have kept my Father's commands and remain in

his love. I have told you this so that my joy may
be in you and that your joy may be complete. My
command is this: Love each other as I have loved
you. Greater love has no one than this: to lay down
one's life for one's friends. You are my friends if you
do what I command. I no longer call you servants,
because a servant does not know his master's
business. Instead, I have called you friends, for
everything that I learned from my Father I have
made known to you. You did not choose me, but I
chose you and appointed you so that you might go
and bear fruit—fruit that will last—and so that
whatever you ask in my name the Father will give
you. This is my command: Love each other."
—JOHN 15:1–17

I don't like waiting: for takeout food, online orders, doctor visits—anything. As I move through the world, things almost never function as expediently as I'd like, and a smoldering restlessness is always rumbling just beneath the surface. Traffic tends to amplify this ever-latent frustration, and I can easily lose my religion in a good gaper delay or unexpected construction area. My continual impatience is compounded by a terrible affliction I suffer (one doctors have yet to properly identify), which causes me to always choose the wrong lane in a backup. Always. The very instant I complete my transition to what is clearly the faster option, it's as if the lane I'd just vacated suddenly glides briskly along and my new one now ceases to move. That is, of course, until I veer back to where I'd been originally seconds ago, upon which that lane once again screeches to a standstill. I soon look ahead into the distance and lament the place farther down the road that I would have occupied had I only stayed put. I watch another driver claim the smooth travel I missed out on, and in a fit of rampant lane envy I pray a pox upon their house—or at least a nice pothole to mess with their alignment.

In this extended sermon in the fifteenth chapter of John's gospel, Jesus uses the word *remain* nearly a dozen times—which makes me think that it's both important and also probably something that isn't easy, or else saying it once or twice would have been enough. Staying put is a profound challenge for many of us, especially if our present is uncomfortable or confusing or turbulent. In such seasons of struggle, it's counterintuitive to not want to get some distance, but Jesus reminds us that growth is sometimes painful and slow. It can't be rushed even when it is both of those things.

There is something sacred and rare about *staying:* about enduring the waiting and trying to stay grounded in love while we face the frustration of what we want to be through with right now. The words of Jesus offer the wise path forward for those of us who don't wait very well: Stay. Love. Repeat.

6) The Voice We Listen To

Then Jesus was led by the Spirit into the wilderness to be tempted by the devil. After fasting forty days and forty nights, he was hungry. The tempter came to him and said, "If you are the Son of God, tell these stones to become bread."

Jesus answered, "It is written: 'Man shall not live on bread alone, but on every word that comes from the mouth of God.'"

Then the devil took him to the holy city and had him stand on the highest point of the temple. "If you are the Son of God," he said, "throw yourself down. For it is written:

"'He will command his angels concerning you, and they will lift you up in their hands, so that you will not strike your foot against a stone.'"

Jesus answered him, "It is also written: 'Do not put the Lord your God to the test.'"

Again, the devil took him to a very high mountain and showed him all the kingdoms of the world and their splendor. "All this I will give you," he said, "if you will bow down and worship me."

Jesus said to him, "Away from me, Satan! For it is written: 'Worship the Lord your God, and serve him only.'"

Then the devil left him, and angels came and attended him.

—MATTHEW 4:1–11

The devil features prominently in the story of the forty-day testing of Jesus in the wilderness in preparation for ministry, which might be a challenge for you theologically. I know it can be for me. Personally, I don't think I've ever heard the devil's voice before; but if I have, it bears a really strong resemblance to my own. It is the taunting voice always hovering in the periphery in my head, waiting for me to make a mistake so it can pounce on the failure and the fear and tell me that I am right to feel insecure. It's the ridiculing voice that often tells me that I'm not good enough, that I'm not doing enough, that I don't have enough; the source of perpetual inadequacy and lack. It is the dismissive voice that (as with Jesus) presses into the tender places of my identity and tries to make me question my worth and work.

My journey with depression and anxiety has been a three-decade season in the wilderness, struggling to hear another voice in the loneliness and the solitary places. It has been a daily, sometimes hourly, act of choosing to listen to the voice that says I am known and loved and held, and to shout down the condemnation when it comes from wherever it comes from. I imagine that on some level, you know what that feels like: to have competing commentary on who you are or who God is and to struggle to believe the better story, especially because the lying voice can be convincing. The account of Jesus' being tested speaks to our vulnerability, to our tendency to listen to the voices of critique and condemnation, and to the power of what we choose to believe even in the moments when belief seems impossible. The declaration of who we are and whose we are is never more necessary than in the wilderness. Today, may you listen to the voice that gives life, and may you believe what it says about you.

7) The Leaving

As Jesus was walking beside the Sea of Galilee, he saw two brothers, Simon called Peter and his brother Andrew. They were casting a net into the lake, for they were fishermen. "Come, follow me," Jesus said, "and I will send you out to fish for people." At once they left their nets and followed him.

Going on from there, he saw two other brothers, James son of Zebedee and his brother John. They were in a boat with their father Zebedee, preparing their nets. Jesus called them, and immediately they left the boat and their father and followed him.

—MATTHEW 4:18–22

I often suffer from buyer's remorse. Well, more accurately, it's more like *chooser's* remorse. If I order dinner at a restaurant, I almost immediately regret that decision, and I soon find myself coveting my neighbor's entrée. If I drive one route somewhere, invariably I lament that path I might have taken, certain it would have been the smoother one. The biggest barrier for me in these frustrating moments is usually the myth I hold about the choice I *didn't* make, of how much better that option would have worked out. These alternative stories are easier to romanticize in my head because they never have to compete with the unpleasant realities of the choices I did make.

I imagine the young men here who left their nets and their boats and their fathers to follow Jesus experienced that frustration from time to time. They had left the familiar to walk with him, abandoning security, safety, and belonging in order to accept the invitation to something audacious but only aspirational. Knowing the way the story unfolds confirms for us that these were wise decisions, but it likely didn't always feel that way from the inside: not when nearly capsized by the wind and the waves, not when targeted by the taunts and threats of Jesus' detractors, and certainly not in the grief following his death. The weight of what they'd left probably felt overwhelming at times.

I think you understand all of this, as your convictions have likely cost you something. Taking the authentic spiritual journey is accepting an invitation to leave: to sever attachments to people or to things we've grown dependent on, communities we've felt defined us, plans we've made for the people we thought we'd be doing life with. Sometimes, as we seek a deeper understanding of God, that will mean leaving behind even the religion we found comfort in. Be encouraged in whatever you let go of in order to follow more closely.

8) The Need and the Knowing

A week later his disciples were in the house again, and Thomas was with them. Though the doors were locked, Jesus came and stood among them and said, "Peace be with you!" Then he said to Thomas, "Put your finger here; see my hands. Reach out your hand and put it into my side. Stop doubting and believe."

Thomas said to him, "My Lord and my God!"
—JOHN 20:26–28

A "doubting Thomas." It's funny how that derisive nickname has persevered two thousand years after this story is said to have occurred, and yet we've never gotten it right about this guy. We always take it for granted that the disciple Thomas was experiencing a blanket lack of belief (which is how we usually apply the phrase), when in reality he simply could not fathom the news of Jesus' resurrection and would not believe without tangible proof, without having evidence he could literally touch with his own hands. I take great comfort in this section of John's gospel for a couple of reasons. For one thing, I see in this bargaining man something I recognize: a struggle to have all the information I want in order to fully embrace this most staggering of mysteries. That in itself is a true encouragement, but I also find solace in Jesus' response to Thomas. It is not scolding or condemning, but accommodating. The ever-compassionate rabbi gives his skeptical student what he needs in order to go all the way with him. He doesn't berate him for his internal barriers to belief, but he meets him there and allows him proximity and experience and knowing, so that Thomas might find peace.

I've heard it said that human beings are either wired for belief or for skepticism: that some of us (who tend to be more emotional) find faith far easier and more natural, while other more cerebral people are constantly battling the intellectual doubt that is their default setting. I'm not sure it's as simple as all that; however, I do know that simple belief has never come easy for me. Taking hold of the reality of Jesus, let alone this rise narrative, seems effortless for lots of people, but for me it's been a meandering road, to say the least. This story with Thomas gives me hope that not only does God know exactly when and why I strain to believe in the times and seasons I do, but also that God is willing to let me have whatever will make the cloudy things clear, eventually. There is almost always a gap between the need and the knowing, but God meets us there in that distance.

9) The Sinner's Dinner

As Jesus went on from there, he saw a man named Matthew sitting at the tax collector's booth. "Follow me," he told him, and Matthew got up and followed him.

While Jesus was having dinner at Matthew's house, many tax collectors and sinners came and ate with him and his disciples. When the Pharisees saw this, they asked his disciples, "Why does your teacher eat with tax collectors and sinners?"

—MATTHEW 9:9–11

When we read the gospels and place ourselves inside the accounts of Jesus' life intersecting with the lives of other human beings two thousand years ago, we tend to give ourselves the most desirable roles. We're usually the earnest disciples or the kindhearted Samaritan, or at worst, we're the humbled prodigal son, coming to his senses after some brief oat-sowing foolishness. We're rarely the vicious, jeering crowds or the apathetic passersby or the jealous brother. I think the more we try to inhabit the skin of the less heroic, less noble characters of these stories, the more expansive a God we're going to come away with, and the better able we're going to be to make space within us for those who may be exempt from our better angels. When I see the people interrogating Jesus' disciples on why Jesus eats with people of questionable conduct and poor reputation, I see myself. I know that whatever the love of God is, I tend to hoard it from people I've decided don't deserve it.

That's the funny thing about who Jesus has to be if he's who we hope he is: He has to be able to out-love us. That means the scandalous dinner invite isn't just for us, it's for the people we despise, for those we disagree with, for everyone who pushes our buttons and boils our blood and twists our insides—and we have to be on board with that. Not only do we need to accept the fact that the table is wide open, but we have to be at the ready with a chair and an extra setting for those we find it most challenging to welcome. If you're at all like me, you've spent a good deal of time and effort crafting what you believe is a compelling, air-tight case against breaking bread with certain people because of the message that would send to them. We don't want people whose religion or politics or behavior are adversarial to ours to "get away with it" by giving them proximity or showing them generosity, and that self-righteousness feels good until we realize that someone somewhere is asking Jesus why he sits with us.

10) A Curious Thing

"Ask and it will be given to you; seek and you will find; knock and the door will be opened to you. For everyone who asks receives; the one who seeks finds; and to the one who knocks, the door will be opened."

—MATTHEW 7:7–8

The words of Jesus can be frustrating, and not just because those words often challenge me to move outside my places of comfort, or demand a self-awareness that feels too invasive, or require a sacrifice that I may not want to make. Sometimes, they simply sound too good to be true. Sometimes, the lofty expectations they produce within my head don't seem to match my here-on-the-ground reality, and that bothers me.

Whether you've been raised in the church or not, you likely know these words about asking and seeking and knocking. Already well into his longest recorded sermon in the gospels, Jesus promises that curious people will be rewarded: that the earnest spiritual search will yield something that makes the journey worth it. Almost matter-of-factly, he assures those listening to him on that hillside (and the rest of us eavesdropping on the gathering two thousand years later) that the cloudy will one day become clear and that all we want to know we will know. I often have difficulty embracing those words, simply because the receiving and the finding and the opened doors are rarely as clear and decisive as they seem in Jesus' declaration. Maybe I'm jealous of people who are certain. I have tiny, fleeting moments of what feels like nebulous confirmation of my hunches or a possible affirmation of my suspicions—but certainly nothing as settled as I'd like. Yet even in the frustration of the unresolved things and the less-than-explicit conclusions of this life, I know that if I can stay in a posture of curiosity, I can be available and prepared to receive the small bits of truth and goodness when they arrive and not miss them.

11) Distance Demons

They went across the lake to the region of the Gerasenes. When Jesus got out of the boat, a man with an impure spirit came from the tombs to meet him. This man lived in the tombs, and no one could bind him anymore, not even with a chain. For he had often been chained hand and foot, but he tore the chains apart and broke the irons on his feet. No one was strong enough to subdue him. Night and day among the tombs and in the hills he would cry out and cut himself with stones.

—MARK 5:1–5

In my three-decade battle with depression, one of the things I've learned about what I call that "lingering sadness" is the way it places distance—both geographic and emotional—between myself and the people around me. When the despair comes and my thoughts spiral into familiar places of criticism and condemnation, I instinctively pull away from others in order to not burden them with my less-than-pleasant mood. Initially I might feel some relief at being spared the awkward interactions, but eventually the lack of interaction brings a loneliness that actually exacerbates the sadness. The silence and solitude force me to fill in the gaps with the voice in my head that tells me I'm a failure or a fraud, and that makes me retreat further. It may or may not be an "unclean spirit," but it's definitely a real pain.

I've read or heard this story hundreds of times in my life, and for the first four hundred or so it was about a guy possessed by a demon and getting released from it amid jagged stones and flying pigs. I don't experience it that way anymore. Now, it's about a scared and hurting human being whose head is a frightening place and whose pain pushes him to an isolation that is not healthy or sustainable. I get that guy. The healing comes to him, and with it comes a pull back into community—or maybe it's the other way around: When he is fully seen and fully known, he is able to find the peace that had eluded him while he was alone. There is something injurious about prolonged separation and something deeply medicinal about community, the way intimacy with other people brings healing like nothing else can. There are certainly times when solitude can restore us, but in the times when our heads become hazardous and despair lingers, the real demon may be the distance that we need to cast out.

12) Death Stinks

Jesus, once more deeply moved, came to the tomb. It was a cave with a stone laid across the entrance. "Take away the stone," he said.

"But, Lord," said Martha, the sister of the dead man, "by this time there is a bad odor, for he has been there four days."

Then Jesus said, "Did I not tell you that if you believe, you will see the glory of God?"

So they took away the stone. Then Jesus looked up and said, "Father, I thank you that you have heard me. I knew that you always hear me, but I said this for the benefit of the people standing here, that they may believe that you sent me."

When he had said this, Jesus called in a loud voice, "Lazarus, come out!" The dead man came out, his hands and feet wrapped with strips of linen, and a cloth around his face.

Jesus said to them, "Take off the grave clothes and let him go."

—JOHN 11:38–44

Ever since my father died, I've really struggled with the story of Lazarus' resurrection. Since then, reading it has been especially painful, because I relive the worst parts of the experience. I recognize a great deal of the account: the depth of the loss, the scalding grief, the utter desperation, the pleading prayers for a miracle, the vacancy left, the hopelessness that sets in afterward. I could fully inhabit that story all the way until the fourth day when the stench of the grave gives way to the fragrant breezes outside it: the moment Jesus calls Lazarus out and they both defy death and there is an unprecedented surprise party for the grieving. Then I become a jealous spectator of someone else's miracle. I'm strangely envious of this family. I didn't get the payoff of that moment. I, too, wanted to see the impossible, to know the knee-rocking surprise of getting someone I love, who'd been taken, returned. Honestly, I didn't expect my father to come walking out of the cemetery four days after we buried him, and I suppose that's part of the tension: We see Jesus do something that we haven't seen him do since, and we wonder why.

I imagine you know what it feels like to not get someone back, to have someone you treasured die and stay dead. Maybe you read this story or even the story of the resurrection of Jesus at the heart of the Lenten journey, the very namesake of this book—and you feel a twinge of anger because you wanted that jubilation a few days later. It would be easy to over-spiritualize a response to you: to talk about resurrection as a metaphor, or to imagine a day when we might be able to see our loved ones again in the hereafter, thereby only postponing our celebratory reunion—but that would be too easy, and it wouldn't honor your grief. Outside of this one man's family, the rest of us have had to live in the loss, to mourn them and to miss them, and to know that on this side of the grave, death really stinks.

13) Sweet Nothings

As Jesus and his disciples were on their way, he came to a village where a woman named Martha opened her home to him. She had a sister called Mary, who sat at the Lord's feet listening to what he said. But Martha was distracted by all the preparations that had to be made. She came to him and asked, "Lord, don't you care that my sister has left me to do the work by myself? Tell her to help me!"

"Martha, Martha," the Lord answered, "you are worried and upset about many things, but few things are needed—or indeed only one. Mary has chosen what is better, and it will not be taken away from her."

—LUKE 10:38–43

Years ago, a pastor told me I had a "dancing mind," which was a kind way of saying I never stopped thinking. This trait has been an asset during brainstorming sessions and planning meetings, where I'm able to deftly cycle through a myriad of options—though it is less helpful when I'm trying to focus or fall asleep, making either task a perpetual challenge, to this day. Having a twirling, gyrating brain is especially difficult in those times when I need to be fully present: when what is most pressing is the moment and the person in front of me. I can easily miss both of them, because I'm usually being pulled out of that moment in and into the countless possibilities of what might be happening elsewhere or what I could be doing or what is coming, I've often failed to witness my life in real time. Part of this Lenten journey, for me, is about the pausing, about a pace that allows for stillness, a place where I can at least dance slow.

I grew up hearing this story of two sisters welcoming Jesus, and learned almost immediately that Mary was the hero, able to simply sit and be with him. I was told in countless sermons to be like Mary. But I've always had a soft spot for Martha because I understand what it is to be "worried and distracted" by the tasks in front of me, to have a well-meaning heart and a mind that gets ahead of it. I realize that she, too, had invited Jesus into her home, and that her intention was to be a gracious and hospitable host. Jesus isn't scolding Martha here, just reminding her and the rest of us that *here* is the only place we are required: here with our family, or our partner, or our friend, or whomever we are sharing this present moment with.

You may not be a victim of a dancing mind; you might have an unsustainable pace or an overcrowded calendar, or an unreasonable expectation for yourself that makes you prone to missing what's in front of you. Today, resist the frenzy and the obligations and the performative—and be *here*.

14) A Wonderful Waste

While [Jesus] was in Bethany, reclining at the table in the home of Simon the Leper, a woman came with an alabaster jar of very expensive perfume, made of pure nard. She broke the jar and poured the perfume on his head.

Some of those present were saying indignantly to one another, "Why this waste of perfume? It could have been sold for more than a year's wages and the money given to the poor." And they rebuked her harshly.

"Leave her alone," said Jesus. "Why are you bothering her? She has done a beautiful thing to me. The poor you will always have with you, and you can help them any time you want. But you will not always have me. She did what she could. She poured perfume on my body beforehand to prepare for my burial. Truly I tell you, wherever the gospel is preached throughout the world, what she has done will also be told, in memory of her."

—Mark 14:3–9

"She did what she could."

These might be my five favorite words attributed to Jesus in the Scriptures. They are spoken about a woman who has broken an expensive bottle of perfume and anointed him, in an audacious act of love that is declared wasteful by those who don't understand her heart. They are words delivered to her detractors but loud enough for her to hear, which is the part that really gets me. They are a public affirmation of her *trying,* one that sees love where others see waste. That can be a challenge in the messy places loving takes us.

As a parent, you get used to feeling like you're perpetually floundering, always wondering if the small things you do mean anything and continually feeling like the pick-ups and the lunches and the heart-to-heart talks are fruitless. This is especially true when your child is struggling or when there is a disconnection between you. In those moments, self-condemnation and self-critique are easy. In all our relationships—whether with children, parents, partners, spouses, or friends—when things feel broken, it can seem as if all that we've done and given has been for nothing. Often, the voices most loudly accusing us are our own. We can so easily forget that there is a beauty in our attempt; and in those moments, we need to remember these five words: I did what I could.

There is something comforting about imagining a God who comes to our defense, who sees our intentions, who understands our desperation, who reminds us that no act of love is ever wasted. I think we all would do better to embrace the reality of such a Maker, one who sees our hearts and celebrates the messes we make.

15) Family Feuds

"Do not suppose that I have come to bring peace to the earth. I did not come to bring peace, but a sword. For I have come to turn

"'a man against his father,

a daughter against her mother,
a daughter-in-law against her mother-in-law—
    a man's enemies will be the members of his own
household.'

"Anyone who loves their father or mother more
than me is not worthy of me; anyone who loves
their son or daughter more than me is not worthy of
me. Whoever does not take up their cross and follow
me is not worthy of me. Whoever finds their life will
lose it, and whoever loses their life for my sake will
find it."

—MATTHEW 10:34–39

"Your convictions are going to be costly."

That's what I hear Jesus saying, as he declares that he came "not to bring peace, but a sword." He isn't saying that war is his agenda, at least not the kind many might imagine. He is promising those gathered in that moment (and those of us still listening today) that if we attempt to fully embrace his invitation to make a more compassionate and equitable world, we are going to experience turbulence—and often from the places we least welcome it: the close places.

Earlier in my journey, I embraced the idea that the relational fractures Jesus was talking about here referred to my poor, faithless family members and friends, that his teachings would drive a wedge between them and me because of their lack of morality and my great virtue. Strangely, the opposite has been true: Those most continually advertising their religion have most often generated the greatest resistance to the kind of radical empathy Jesus embodied—and that in turn has expanded the divide between us.

I now see that Jesus wasn't declaring that peace wasn't his plan, simply that the greater kind of wholeness he was bringing to vulnerable and oppressed people (and to the world because of this) necessitated a disruption for those who benefitted from the existing inequities—and he expected us to be on the front lines of that. This means that the audacious work of Jesus may be most rejected by professed Christians. Inventorying the schisms between me and many people close to me in recent years, I've begun to see them as part of the price of speaking with clarity and working for justice; that even though I grieve the separations and disconnections, I can see them as *swords* that are doing something bigger and ultimately redemptive.

I'm not sure if you've suffered relationally as you've pursued a religion that makes a way for more people, but I want to encourage you to be willing to. It isn't necessarily a sign that you're getting anything wrong. In fact, the pushback—by those who claim ownership of Jesus—may be confirmation that you're getting the most important things right.

16) The Forty-First Day

> *Jesus, full of the Holy Spirit, left the Jordan and was led by the Spirit into the wilderness, where for forty days he was tempted by the devil. He ate nothing during those days, and at the end of them he was hungry.*
>
> *The devil said to him, "If you are the Son of God, tell this stone to become bread." Jesus answered, "It is written: 'Man shall not live on bread alone.'"*

The devil led him up to a high place and showed him in an instant all the kingdoms of the world. And he said to him, "I will give you all their authority and splendor; it has been given to me, and I can give it to anyone I want to. If you worship me, it will all be yours."

Jesus answered, "It is written: 'Worship the Lord your God and serve him only.'"

The devil led him to Jerusalem and had him stand on the highest point of the temple. "If you are the Son of God," he said, "throw yourself down from here. For it is written:

"'He will command his angels concerning you
*   to guard you carefully;*
they will lift you up in their hands,
*   so that you will not strike your foot against a stone.'"*

Jesus answered, "It is said: 'Do not put the Lord your God to the test.'"

When the devil had finished all this tempting, he left him until an opportune time.

—LUKE 4:1–13

The gospel writer Luke describes Jesus' being tested in the wilderness for forty days before his public ministry: forty days of loneliness, of hunger, of vulnerability. The Old Testament tells us that for forty years the Israelites wandered in search of a promised land of abundance, rest, and safety. There are many parallels in these in-between journeys, yet where the former knew the duration of the challenge ahead before beginning, the latter did not. I imagine that made a huge difference. The wilderness seasons of our lives rarely come with expiration dates in advance. They usually don't tell us beforehand (or even as we are enduring them) that they are finite, that our suffering is perishable and temporary, that the victory is ultimately in outlasting them, in waiting on a change of circumstance. If the difficult journeys did come with such disclaimers, weathering them might be a bit easier. We could simply count the days and be certain relief was coming.

The big lie that depression and grief and fear all tell us is a similar one: that this terrible present is now our permanent default condition, that we will always feel the way we feel today. They fool us into believing there will not be a forty-first day or a forty-first year—but that is untrue. The wilderness experiences of Jesus and of the Israelites remind us that our moments of testing never have the last word. Somewhere on the horizon, there always exists a day when we step out of the struggle and the wandering and into a milk and honey space where the clarity that seems elusive right now does indeed arrive. It doesn't take away the severity of the current pain, but it does reassure us that it will not be permanent.

Be encouraged in the waiting. Your forty-first day is coming.

17) Fears and False Stories

When the disciples saw him walking on the lake, they were terrified. "It's a ghost," they said, and cried out in fear.

But Jesus immediately said to them: "Take courage! It is I. Don't be afraid."

"Lord, if it's you," Peter replied, "tell me to come to you on the water."

—MATTHEW 14:26–28

In the work I do as a pastor, caregiver, and consultant, people tell me things they don't feel they can tell anyone else. Often, when I meet people in my travels on speaking tours, we don't necessarily have a lot of time together. They might come up before or after a talk and tell me something deeply personal about a conflict with another person. In a quick moment and without knowing any of their backstory, they're hoping I can give them something they can take home to help them.

Here's what I tell them: Look for the fears and the false stories. Find out what people are afraid of, and figure out why those fears might be misplaced or addressed—because no one is at their best when they're terrified. This is true of us as well. When we're in conflict with other people—whether we're debating politics or religions, finances or work problems, parenting issues or strong opinions on any topic—the other person is almost always afraid of something, and that fear drives them (and us) to hold or defend a certain position. Many times, people's fears are well-founded, but often those fears are based on a false story: a set of believed circumstances or accepted truths that aren't always accurate. In our interactions with them, we might be able to give them a perspective they don't have—not to win an argument or change their minds, but to take away their fear. I believe that in this life, we're given the choice to be peace givers or fear bringers: to either make other people's journeys easier or provide greater turbulence for them. One of the primary ways we can be peace givers is by helping them to be less afraid than they are.

Today, try looking for the fear and false stories and see if that doesn't change how you interact with people.

18) The Hands That Heal

While Jesus was in one of the towns, a man came along who was covered with leprosy. When he saw Jesus, he fell with his face to the ground and begged him, "Lord, if you are willing, you can make me clean."

Jesus reached out his hand and touched the man. "I am willing," he said. "Be clean!" And immediately the leprosy left him.

Then Jesus ordered him, "Don't tell anyone, but go, show yourself to the priest and offer the sacrifices that Moses commanded for your cleansing, as a testimony to them."

Yet the news about him spread all the more, so that crowds of people came to hear him and to be healed of their sicknesses. But Jesus often withdrew to lonely places and prayed.

—Luke 5:12–16

In the throes of the pandemic, I was asked to preside over a dear friend's funeral. Had it been almost anyone else I'd have said no, but she was there for me throughout my life in ways few people had been, and I felt I now needed to be there for her and her family. I accepted, with the caveats that I would need to be masked at all times, that I would be strictly distancing—and above all, that I would not be able to have physical contact with anyone, including her children and husband, who I loved and hadn't seen in years. They agreed. Though I'd tried to mentally prepare myself beforehand, I wasn't ready for the emotional disorientation of greeting a grieving family who'd lost someone they adored, while being unable to physically embrace them. It seemed unnatural to feel so deeply without expressing that with proximity.

One of the strangest aspects of the prolonged isolation of the health crisis was the way it took away *touch* from our lives. Other than the people we happened to live with, most of us went more than a year without physical contact with another human being. Without a high five or a hug or a handshake or a kiss, we all felt the weight of that distance. We've come through this year apart from people with a deeper appreciation for the way we interact with other human beings physically and how integral it is to our sense of connection and feelings of intimacy.

Luke describes the way Jesus heals a man with leprosy by touching him, though he didn't need to do that. Surely he could have just proclaimed the sick man well, but I think Jesus gave him something he'd been without for a long time: a touch that reminded him of his humanity. I imagine that alone was medicinal. We may not be able to miraculously heal people's physical conditions with the touch of our hands, but we can tend to the wounds of loneliness and sadness and fear of the world in ways that matter.

19) Mystery Loves Company

Again he said, "What shall we say the kingdom of God is like, or what parable shall we use to describe it? It is like a mustard seed, which is the smallest of all seeds on earth. Yet when planted, it grows and becomes the largest of all garden plants, with such big branches that the birds can perch in its shade."

With many similar parables Jesus spoke the word to them, as much as they could understand. He did not say anything to them without using a parable. But when he was alone with his own disciples, he explained everything.

—M<small>ARK</small> 4:30–34

Years ago, I was speaking at a facility run by one of the most famous evangelists in the world. In the weeks approaching the event I agonized over what I could possibly offer those gathered, as my feeble attempts at pithy wisdom would surely pale in comparison to the astute reflections they'd been spoiled by. One morning, a thought occurred to me: *He doesn't know any more than you do.* Yes, he'd had more theological education and had been raised surrounded by religion and had spoken to hundreds of thousands of people—but in the end, he was still left with incompletes to the greatest questions of this life. There was still a massive gap between what he suspected and what he knew. This realization was emotionally emancipating. There was no comparison sickness anymore, no imposter syndrome, no feeling as though my spiritual journey was somehow less-than. I could rest on the level ground of uncertainty.

I'm jealous of the disciples in this passage. I want to sit with Jesus and have him clearly explain spirituality to me so that the mystery is gone, so that all the unsettled things become still, so that the cloudiness in my head is cleared—but that's rarified air, reserved only for a dozen or so human beings. The rest of us have to do our best to sift through the words and ask the questions and make our best guess at how all this stuff gets made real. The bad news of this truth is that we're always going to be working with incomplete information no matter how much we learn and how earnest our search. The good news is that in this great not knowing, we are in really good company.

20) Invitation to Play

*[Jesus] called a little child to him, and placed
the child among them. And he said: "Truly I tell
you, unless you change and become like little
children, you will never enter the kingdom of
heaven. Therefore, whoever takes the lowly position
of this child is the greatest in the kingdom of
heaven."*

—MATTHEW 18:2–4

Years ago, we took our kids to a local indoor play
area, one of those giant human hamster cages where
parents deposit their offspring for an hour or so, only
briefly catching glimpses of them in the small portholes
of giant plastic tubes or maneuvering awkwardly in a
massive net above them, like trapped crabs just pulled
up from the ocean. My daughter bounded through the
playground entrance and immediately began removing
her shoes, while our son (who was nearly five years older)
was greeted with a sign that read, *You must be shorter than
this line to enter*—and he was not. In the way such things
are exaggerated in a young mind, this seemed to be a
monumental setback: being deemed too grown to enter
the play area, yet really wanting to.

I've never quite known what Jesus meant about
our needing to become like little children to enter the
kingdom, but I think it has something to do with the
way we approach the very idea of God, how we navigate
the not-knowing, how able we are to keep dreaming.
As adults, when we experience a crisis of faith or have
moments of doubt or have outgrown an old belief, it's
easy to be frustrated at everything we aren't able to figure

out. We can see the unknowns as a struggle rather than an adventure. Children don't seem intimidated by mystery in that way. They don't feel angst around it. They are prone to wonder. The older I've gotten, the more I've been trying to embrace the *unfigureoutable* things and make peace with the incompletes.

The kingdom is an invitation to play. You must be this curious to enter.

21) Surprise Party

When Jesus had finished saying all this to the people who were listening, he entered Capernaum. There a centurion's servant, whom his master valued highly, was sick and about to die. The centurion heard of Jesus and sent some elders of the Jews to him, asking him to come and heal his servant. When they came to Jesus, they pleaded earnestly with him, "This man deserves to have you do this, because he loves our nation and has built our synagogue." So Jesus went with them.

He was not far from the house when the centurion sent friends to say to him: "Lord, don't trouble yourself, for I do not deserve to have you come under my roof. That is why I did not even consider myself worthy to come to you. But say the word, and my servant will be healed. For I myself am a man under authority, with soldiers under me. I tell this one, 'Go,' and he goes; and that one, 'Come,' and he comes. I say to my servant, 'Do this,' and he does it."

When Jesus heard this, he was amazed at him, and turning to the crowd following him, he said, "I tell you, I have not found such great faith even in Israel." Then the men who had been sent returned to the house and found the servant well.

—LUKE 7:1–10

Fraud. Failure. Imposter. Once these labels stick to us, they are nearly impossible to remove, because the voice that declares them is so often our own. We aren't just our worst critics, but the most informed ones. Since we're intimately aware of who we are and what we think and where we've faltered, self-condemnation is especially easy. Where others see us less critically or give us the benefit of the doubt or simply appreciate us without judgment, we know better, and so we rarely respond with any mercy or gratitude for ourselves. This usually leaves us with the enduring narrative of our deficiencies disqualifying us to be the leader, the parent, the friend, the human that we'd like to be. That's a pretty sad way to spend this journey.

I love the subversive surprises of the four gospel accounts: A faithful centurion. A good Samaritan. A tax collector disciple. A pariah-turned-preacher. The unexpected heroes throughout scripture point to the beautiful inversion at the heart of the bigger story: that of a humble servant savior who doesn't come armed with shield and sword but with fish and bread, who invites people into a counterintuitive movement that will not conquer by force but win over with kindness. The gospel is the story of the losers and freaks and outcasts coming to do what the religious experts and the righteous perfect people could not, and that should be such good news to those of us who feel as if we're never quite measuring up. What if we saw ourselves as the unlikely hero in a plot twist moment? What if we imagined ourselves as perfectly prepared and positioned to do and be everything we'd like to, even as terribly imperfect as we are? Maybe the precedent has already been set. Maybe we are frauds, failures, and imposters—and maybe we're the hero we least expect.

22) The Prayer You Can Pray

"And when you pray, do not be like the hypocrites, for they love to pray standing in the synagogues and on the street corners to be seen by others. Truly I tell you, they have received their reward in full. But when you pray, go into your room, close the door and pray to your Father, who is unseen. Then your Father, who sees what is done in secret, will reward you. And when you pray, do not keep on babbling like pagans, for they think they will be heard because of their many words."

—MATTHEW 6:5–7

Confession: I get self-conscious writing greeting cards. It's a strange kind of writer's performance anxiety, I guess. As someone whose life's work is the arranging of words, I feel expected to come up with something especially profound on special occasions. I had a similar problem, back when I was a working artist, anytime I had to play *Pictionary*. I figured people would be disappointed if my twelve-second sketch of a cruise ship or a skyscraper didn't include the proper two-point perspective.

As a Christian, I used to think I needed to impress God with my prayers. I grew more and more self-aware when praying, whether out loud or in my head, trying to string together words that sounded properly religious or especially astute, as if God would be in awe of them. (I suppose I was trying to impress the people who could hear those prayers, more than anything.) One day, I realized that if God was indeed God, then God created all those words and nothing I could say would really be a revelation. There was no impressing to be done. Not only could God not be impressed, but God could not be fooled, either. No matter the state of my belief or the condition of my heart, God could handle that—and anything less than authenticity was a waste of energy. So I started praying whatever prayer I could.

Other people tend to be uncomfortable with our doubts, our vacillation, and our messy, unsteady faith—but fortunately, the spiritual journey isn't about impressing those people. In fact, it isn't about impressing God. God is unimpressible. Thankfully, whoever and whatever God is can bear the weight of our questions, takes no offense at our uncertainty, and welcomes the unadorned words from honest hearts. Today, pray whatever prayer you can pray, and know it is perfectly stated.

23) The Un-Missed Life

"All things have been committed to me by my Father. No one knows the Son except the Father, and no one knows the Father except the Son and those to whom the Son chooses to reveal him.

"Come to me, all you who are weary and burdened, and I will give you rest. Take my yoke upon you and learn from me, for I am gentle and humble in heart, and you will find rest for your souls."

—MATTHEW 11:27–29

A couple of summers ago we decided to take a spontaneous Saturday trip to the beach, as we're fortunate enough to live just a two-hour drive from the North Carolina coast. We woke up and tossed the essentials (including children) into the back of the car, and by lunchtime we were feeling the glorious sting of scalding hot sand beneath our feet.

Just as we were getting out of the car, I made what (for me) was a split-second, paradigm-shifting decision: I left my phone behind. It may not sound monumental, but it mattered. You see, I've been noticing that I've been missing something lately, something fleeting and rare and priceless—something that I should be urgently, obsessively consumed with. I've been missing *Life*. So many times, my attention is pulled from the people I'm with and the place where I'm standing.

That day on beach, I decided to try living life with those who were with me, instead of artistically documenting it for those who were not. Something really great happened in me during those few hours. For a brief afternoon, I was fully present for my own life, and fully present to those around me. I was one hundred percent *there*. Unfettered by the false urgency of somewhere else, I moved more slowly and purposefully. My heart and mind stopped racing, simply taking in the breathtaking panorama in front of me instead of trying to capture it for people hundreds of miles away. Without my head perpetually bowed into the palms of my hands, I saw everything, for the first time in a long time. I may have missed some really great photo opportunities that afternoon. I may have missed the quick high of the momentary attention from people who are relatively strangers—but I know what I didn't miss. That afternoon, I didn't miss my life as it was happening. Don't miss yours.

24) The Thing of Value

*"The kingdom of heaven is like treasure hidden in
a field. When a man found it, he hid it again, and
then in his joy went and sold all he had and bought
that field.*

*"Again, the kingdom of heaven is like a merchant
looking for fine pearls. When he found one of great
value, he went away and sold everything he had and
bought it."*

—MATTHEW 13:44–46

Yesterday, I was talking with an old friend, and our
conversation drifted into spirituality. I expected that
we were going to discuss our slightly differing faith
perspectives on the issue at hand, but he surprised me. He
said, "I gave that religious stuff up years ago, and it was
the best decision I ever made." He wasn't looking down
on me or ridiculing me or intentionally belittling me. He
just acted as if he'd outgrown something I still hadn't—
which made me feel looked down upon and ridiculed
and belittled. More than anything, I kind of envied him
because he seemed freer than me, at least on the surface.
He seemed to have come to a conclusion that simplified
his daily existence. The big questions and theological
wrestling and existential crises that I've grown so used to
are no longer issues for him. He is simply present in the
moment, without needing religion to make sense of it.

There are days when I wonder if faith is worth it, days
when all the wondering and questioning and striving feel
rather foolish, especially when I encounter human beings
I respect who believe it isn't. With the growing number
of people who don't claim a religious worldview, being

someone who still believes can begin to make you feel as if you're clinging to something antiquated or obsolete—or, at best, as if you are one of the last of a severely endangered species. Jesus' teaching often speaks to this tension between what most people value and what spiritual people value, describing an elusive, life-giving road that few people find.

In these parables, Jesus gives us this wonderful image of a man who finds a hidden treasure that is both invisible to everyone else and worth everything. The man is not necessarily in step with the people around him, with those who only see a field and not the invaluable. Jesus doesn't describe the man's arrogance or selfishness or wisdom, but his joy at the discovery he has made and how the sacrifice pales compared to what he receives. I am reminded of the joy I have encountered along this journey: moments of profound meaning and deep gratitude that brought me here and sustain me. Today, think about what faith has cost you and what it has given you—and realize the riches you possess.

25) Sacred Intersections

> *"They also will answer, 'Lord, when did we see you hungry or thirsty or a stranger or needing clothes or sick or in prison, and did not help you?'*
>
> *"He will reply, 'Truly I tell you, whatever you did not do for one of the least of these, you did not do for me.'"*
>
> —Matthew 25:44–45

One summer afternoon nearly two decades ago, I was walking down a crowded Philadelphia street and just about to enter the crosswalk when the sky quickly turned black and the clouds opened up, sending a sudden downpour on everything. Like everyone around me, I started sprinting for the cover of the closest storefront awning—but out of the corner of my eye I noticed a man in an electric wheelchair on the sidewalk, being pelted with rain and struggling to get a poncho over his head. I instinctively ran to him and helped him get the blue plastic over his shoulder, gently nudged his head through the hole, and placed the hood on his head. He looked up and gave me a wide smile, and I smiled back and continued on. All these years later, I still remember that moment, not because it made me feel superior or righteous, but because it made me feel useful. And that usefulness is one of the greatest gifts we get here. That day, I hadn't done anything extraordinary in any quantifiable measure. I simply encountered someone who was getting rained on, and I was able to help him stay dry; that was it. The moment reinforced for me that the spiritual journey isn't about ability but availability; it's about being attentive, present, and willing, and knowing that we are always equipped to be a help.

Jesus fed people, not because it boosted his ego, but because they were hungry and he knew what that felt like. He didn't heal people to show how kind he was, but because his body was no stranger to pain and he wanted to spare others that same injury. When he instructs us to love the least and promises that he inhabits their bodies, he gives us a two-fold blessing: We *encounter him* in the human being we care for, and we *incarnate him* in our actions. Their humanity presses up against our own, and whatever God is shows up in that intersection. Countless times in this day you will have the opportunity to do something deeply spiritual: In some small, seemingly ordinary way, you can help keep the rain off someone and come face to face with the best of yourself. Stay available.

26) Tough Questions and Easy Answers

> *Once when Jesus was praying in private and his*
> *disciples were with him, he asked them, "Who do*
> *the crowds say I am?"*
>
> *They replied, "Some say John the Baptist; others say*
> *Elijah; and still others, that one of the prophets of*
> *long ago has come back to life."*
>
> *"But what about you?" he asked. "Who do you say*
> *I am?"*
>
> *Peter answered, "God's Messiah."*
>
> —LUKE 9:18–20

Back when I was a youth pastor, we used to have a joke about answering Sunday School questions: When in doubt, just say "Jesus," and you have a decent shot at being right. And if Jesus *wasn't* the answer, you could get within "six degrees of separation" with whatever the correct response was, and still be roundabout right. Back then, faith was simpler for me in so many ways. I had a tidy arrangement of doctrines and platitudes and scripture passages that gave me a false sense of certainty, regardless of how difficult the question or how challenging the issue in front of me. My perceived surety left me unfazed. I basically knew the answer involved Jesus on some level, and because of that I used to have a great deal of arrogance about what I said I believed—until gradually I realized how little of it I actually believed. Suddenly, I became much humbler.

This passage from Luke's gospel—where Jesus asks his disciples the *big question*, "Who do you say I am?"—was, for me, always about being theologically right: about having the correct answer and believing the proper thing and feeling morally superior to so many who'd gotten it wrong. Lately, when I read it, I see the juxtaposition between those few who have proximity and the crowd who sit at a distance. I see Jesus pulling the curious in close and saying, "There's a lot of talk about me out there. What are they saying?" and following up with, "So, what have *you* seen?" I see a validation of their testimony, and I feel better resting in mine. Though I don't have the certainty I once did, I still think it all connects to Jesus somehow: that if I stay close and stay curious, I'll be able to have the answers that allude me. I don't have any easy answers, but I continue to lean in to find whatever ones I can.

27) Lover, Runner, Fighter

> In the temple courts [Jesus] found people selling
> cattle, sheep and doves, and others sitting at tables
> exchanging money. So he made a whip out of cords,
> and drove all from the temple courts, both sheep and
> cattle; he scattered the coins of the money changers
> and overturned their tables. To those who sold doves
> he said, "Get these out of here! Stop turning my
> Father's house into a market!"
>
> —JOHN 2:14–16

We often reference the story of Jesus' clearing the temple as a way of justifying anger (I know I do), and certainly it reminds us that anger and goodness aren't mutually exclusive. Yet it's important to realize that though this more demonstrative expression isn't out of character for Jesus, it's not commonplace, either. This wasn't Jesus' default setting. This was selective outrage.

It's easy for compassionate human beings to develop *outrage addiction*. We can become so conditioned to the battles and the wars that we become dependent on them, falling into a pattern of opposition in which we continually seek information that keeps us in. Over the last year you may have actively pushed back against a politician or a party or a piece of legislation or a religious movement, and now even if that has been resolved you can't figure out how to stop fighting.

You've probably heard that expression, "I'm a lover not a fighter." I always used to joke, "I'm a runner, then a lover, then a fighter." And I think that perfectly encapsulates how I'd like you to approach the emotional and physical toll of this work: By fighting, loving, and running. One of the keys to fighting outrage addiction and the fatigue of the fight is in noticing our energy orientation: realizing where our energies are being expended, where we are putting our resources, and where we are directing our attention— and making sure we have diversity of experience. Sometimes we turn over tables and chase away the opportunists, and other times we set tables and feed those who are most vulnerable. If we exist only in a battle posture and only fight, we are going to become negative and exhausted and bitter.

Think about your resource allotment and your energy orientation today. Spend some time fighting, some time loving, and, when you're tired, some time running from it all.

28) A Worrisome Sin

Then Jesus said to his disciples: "Therefore I tell you, do not worry about your life, what you will eat; or about your body, what you will wear. For life is more than food, and the body more than clothes. Consider the ravens: They do not sow or reap, they have no storeroom or barn; yet God feeds them. And how much more valuable you are than birds! Who of you by worrying can add a single hour to your life? Since you cannot do this very little thing, why do you worry about the rest?"

—LUKE 12:22–26

This morning, a friend of mine posted on social media that she didn't get much sleep last night, but "did manage to get in a solid six hours of anxiety." I erupted in laughter because I understood her more than I wish I did. Although I'm usually good for worry at any time of the day, there's something about the darkness that tends to magnify my fears and accelerate the whirlwind in my head. The small concerns cast far larger shadows than they should, and the big things become almost insurmountable. I've always known this wasn't healthy, but I've never considered it immoral. Maybe I should.

Thou shalt not worry.

That's essentially the message from Jesus to those listening here in this passage, which includes you and me encountering his words right now. He isn't gently suggesting we avoid worry if we can manage it, or that it would be great if we could make an attempt at a quieted mind. It feels as much like a command as any instruction in the Bible, which is actually refreshing: to think about worry as a spiritual hazard that Jesus wants us to run from—not because we'll make God angry if we don't (we can usually do guilt without much encouragement), but because we will be missing the peace that we deserve and are designed to have. Jesus is essentially saying, "If God is God and you are created by and connected to God, you should breathe easy in this life." And if we can believe this is true in the waking light of the morning—that we are held and cared for and deserving of a joyous exhale—then we should claim it in the dark hours, too. Peace is obedience.

29) Things to Let Go Of

And he told them this parable: "The ground of a certain rich man yielded an abundant harvest. He thought to himself, 'What shall I do? I have no place to store my crops.'

"Then he said, 'This is what I'll do. I will tear down my barns and build bigger ones, and there I will store my surplus grain. And I'll say to myself, "You have plenty of grain laid up for many years. Take life easy; eat, drink and be merry."'

"But God said to him, 'You fool! This very night your life will be demanded from you. Then who will get what you have prepared for yourself?'"
—LUKE 12:16–20

I drove past two new multi-story storage facilities near my home (which is apparently surrounded by a lot of other homes, all outgrowing their capacity for stuff and spilling over into these concrete cathedrals). I stared at the massive rows of sliding metal doors, trying to imagine what was in there and wondering if it was worth what it cost its owners to have. As I did, I remembered the words of Jesus in this scripture passage about "building bigger barns" and was struck by how vivid a description he provided two thousand years ago. It got me thinking about the way I spend the two primary resources of money and time, about the economy of my days.

My friend, poet and activist Genesis Be, has a movement called *People Not Things*. That phrase is such an eloquent declaration of something we know is true yet have a really difficult time embodying, because the things are always competing with people for our heart space. The things are seductive and persistent. We believe all sorts of lies about the things: that they will validate us or declare our lives meaningful or give us permanent respite from our nagging restlessness—but the things lie, don't they? One of the realities of the things is that they will always cost us time: We need to spend the latter in order to acquire the former—and that means someone loses time with us.

Until recently I didn't see the connection between the parable of the bigger barn builder and Jesus' command to love God and others. The caution against continually upsizing isn't only because this will leave us with more financial resources to honor God—but also that we will have more of our very finite time with invaluable people.

30) Steps and Sinking

Immediately Jesus made the disciples get into the boat and go on ahead of him to the other side, while he dismissed the crowd. After he had dismissed them, he went up on a mountainside by himself to pray. Later that night, he was there alone, and the boat was already a considerable distance from land, buffeted by the waves because the wind was against it.

Shortly before dawn Jesus went out to them, walking on the lake. When the disciples saw him walking on the lake, they were terrified. "It's a ghost," they said, and cried out in fear.

*But Jesus immediately said to them: "Take
courage! It is I. Don't be afraid."*

*"Lord, if it's you," Peter replied, "tell me to come to
you on the water."*

"Come," he said.

*Then Peter got down out of the boat, walked on the
water and came toward Jesus. But when he saw the
wind, he was afraid and, beginning to sink, cried
out, "Lord, save me!"*

*Immediately Jesus reached out his hand and caught
him. "You of little faith," he said, "why did you
doubt?"*

*And when they climbed into the boat, the wind died
down. Then those who were in the boat worshiped
him, saying, "Truly you are the Son of God."*
—MATTHEW 14:22–33

Peter has always been an encouraging character to
me. He has a passionate, aspirational faith paired with an
outsized heart permanently affixed to his sleeve, which
often makes him a walking contradiction of big words
and shallow deeds. I recognize myself in that disconnect,
the cavernous gap between what I intend to do and what
I often end up doing. Throughout the gospel stories, there
is such humanity in the precipitous rise and fall of his
time alongside Jesus: moments of both incredible courage
and staggering cowardice—and sometimes within a few
minutes of one another. That inconsistency is familiar
and comforting.

In these moments in the boat recorded by Matthew,
we witness Peter's literal rise and fall: weightless upon
the surface of the water and panic-stricken as he sinks
beneath it. That, too, is familiar ground. This story is often

told highlighting Peter's lack of faith and his descent into the depths; but for me it's about those few seconds of his glorious elevation, of feeling for a second what it is to transcend the tumult of this place and see something else on the horizon. I imagine those steps sustained him for the remainder of his life. Some days I wonder why I am still a person of faith, and I think it's because I know that I can be wildly inconsistent and still be on my way. It's also because there have been those elevated steps upon the water that have never left me. I wonder what they are for you—the moments where you felt weightless and wide-eyed. Today, rest in your inconsistency, make peace with your failures, and treasure the steps upon the water when you get them.

31) Seen and Set Free

Then, leaving her water jar, the woman went back to the town and said to the people, "Come, see a man who told me everything I ever did. Could this be the Messiah?" They came out of the town and made their way toward him.

—JOHN 4:28–30

When I was younger, Christmas used to be doubly worrisome. Like many children, I grew up believing that God (like Santa Claus) was always watching me and (also like Santa Claus) was keeping track of my good and bad deeds, waiting to reward or punish me based on the final tally. The big difference between my two supernatural stalkers was that with Saint Nick the worst I could do was a lump of coal in my stocking (until the following year when I could redeem myself), while God could surround me with lakes of fire and burning sulfur for all eternity. Either way, I always felt like I was being watched by someone who was out to catch me failing, which can really mess with a third-grade mind.

I carried that fear of the eyes of God who wanted to squash me for a long time, and religious people were more than happy to stoke those hell fires to get me to be a good boy—or else. Then I remember coming across this passage as a college student. It shook me to my core in the best of ways: a woman with a past she'd worked hard to hide, a less-than-sterling story she was trying to overcome, and a Jesus who saw it all and wasn't fazed in the least. He shows her how well he knows her, and in that truth she is not frightened, but set free. Sometime after this encounter with Jesus, the writer John records the woman's joyous testimony to the people of her town: "Come see a man who told me everything I ever did." They're some of my favorite words in scripture.

I found in this passage a God who knew me but whose knowledge wasn't weaponized against me. Being seen by God gave me a sense of home, of being found, of acceptance that made me feel that I had an ally in Jesus and not an adversary. The God I know now is not cataloging my actions in order to scare me into belief or acceptable behavior, but giving me a place to live fully known and fully loved.

32) Carried People

One day Jesus was teaching, and Pharisees and teachers of the law were sitting there. They had come from every village of Galilee and from Judea and Jerusalem. And the power of the Lord was with

Jesus to heal the sick. Some men came carrying a
paralyzed man on a mat and tried to take him into
the house to lay him before Jesus. When they could
not find a way to do this because of the crowd, they
went up on the roof and lowered him on his mat
through the tiles into the middle of the crowd, right
in front of Jesus.

When Jesus saw their faith, he said, "Friend, your
sins are forgiven."

—LUKE 5:17–20

As I mentioned earlier, I've battled depression for a
couple of decades, and I'm grateful for that. Not necessarily
for my illness, but grateful because the fact that I'm still
here battling means I'm still here, while so many are not.
I think about people in my life, or those I've known from
a distance, whose stories have ended while I'm here still
co-writing mine. There are reasons for this, many which
I'll never really understand, but some that are easy to
identify. One reason I'm still here is that I have often been
carried by the love of good people. I've been fortunate to
share life with human beings who showed up at the right
time and, through their generosity or kindness or humor,
simply saved me.

For this reason, the account of a man being brought to
Jesus by his friends has always been meaningful, because
it reminds me of how powerful true community is in
helping us when we exhaust our resources, the way it fills
in the gaps and sustains us in the painful seasons. There
is a beautiful absurdity in the image of a group of people
so desperate to help a man they love that they climb on
top of a house, dismantle the roof, and lower him down to
Jesus. Audacious stuff. I used to wonder what the carried
man felt in those moments as he descended through the

ceiling, but after enduring years of illness, I understand. I know what it is to be helpless and then helped. I know how it feels to be that loved. The community of carriers hasn't just allowed me to overcome the overwhelming, but it's taught me how to be one of those determined friends, too. I want to be the kind of friend who carries someone when they need to be carried. I want to be the kind of friend who will not be dissuaded by the crowd. I want to be the kind of friend who rises to the rooftops and does something outrageous so that someone else can know healing. In the song "One," by the band U2, Bono sings one of the trust prayers of ascension: "We get to carry each other."[1] Be a carrier when you can, but allow yourself the blessing of being carried, too.

33) Free Meals

Then Jesus said to his host, "When you give a luncheon or dinner, do not invite your friends, your brothers or sisters, your relatives, or your rich neighbors; if you do, they may invite you back and so you will be repaid. But when you give a banquet, invite the poor, the crippled, the lame, the blind, and you will be blessed. Although they cannot repay you, you will be repaid at the resurrection of the righteous."

—LUKE 14:12–14

Compassion doesn't really make a lot of sense, at least not to our modern, Westernized brains. Most of us are taught to determine the merit of an act based on the

---

[1] U2, "One," track 3 on *Achtung Baby,* Island Records, 1991, CD.

balance between risk and reward: on getting something commensurate with the effort required. Raised in a culture of competitive consumerism, in which we often evaluate and are evaluated by others based on what we own or make or have done, it feels counterintuitive to do something when there is no obvious reward. Even our acts of kindness are often tinged by the question of what the upside will be: Will we be seen in a more flattering light as a result? Will this provide some possible benefit down the road? Do we get an ego boost by doing it? If the answer to any of those question is *no,* it can be easy to simply avoid the inconveniences often caused by kindness. That's probably why so many people gravitate toward self-centeredness, or at least self-preservation—and why narcissism is a tempting default position in a dog-eat-dog society that tells us we are the center of the universe. As usual, Jesus flips things upside down and invites us to another, far better path.

In the kingdom economy of generosity, the *payment* is in the act itself, in being useful in someone else's sustenance or healing or elevation. Nothing else is needed: no applause, no kudos, no praise from the crowd, no advantage. The inverted race Jesus invites us to run is one in which to win is to come in last: to be the servant of all, the person taking the lowest place, the host to those rarely treated with hospitality. His words here to a room full of competitors jockeying for position and striving to be seen (people we can recognize very well) speak not only to doing the right thing but to doing it for the right reason: to be part of someone else's rise without any other benefit. Today, check your motives and challenge yourself not to worry about the upside of a kind act, but to see the kindness as the upside.

34) The Beauty in Being Visible

Then they came to Jericho. As Jesus and his disciples, together with a large crowd, were leaving the city, a blind man, Bartimaeus (which means "son of Timaeus"), was sitting by the roadside begging. When he heard that it was Jesus of Nazareth, he began to shout, "Jesus, Son of David, have mercy on me!"

Many rebuked him and told him to be quiet, but he shouted all the more, "Son of David, have mercy on me!"

Jesus stopped and said, "Call him."

So they called to the blind man, "Cheer up! On your feet! He's calling you." Throwing his cloak aside, he jumped to his feet and came to Jesus.

"What do you want me to do for you?" Jesus asked him.

The blind man said, "Rabbi, I want to see."

"Go," said Jesus, "your faith has healed you." Immediately he received his sight and followed Jesus along the road.

—MARK 10:46–52

I'll never forget an email I received from an eleventh-grade girl who just a couple of days earlier had attended the opening day student gathering at our North Carolina church along with her younger brother. Out of the hundreds of teenagers I'd encountered that night, I'd remembered meeting them because of how horribly I thought our exchange had gone. The two stood along the back wall the entire night, arms crossed, unsmiling, visibly telegraphing their discomfort, and this caught my attention. I approached them and attempted to make conversation, hoping to find the right words or to plow through their formidable defenses, but to seemingly no avail. After wiping away a substantial wave of flop sweat from my brow, I slinked away believing I'd failed to make them feel welcome.

But the girl's email described our conversation that night and concluded with her relaying the difficulty they'd experienced at previous churches, their resistance to being there, and their parents' insistence that they attend. She wrote, "I appreciate you taking the time to see us and come talk to us. It made a difference. You made me feel visible, and I rarely feel visible, so thank you."

In this passage, I love the words attributed to the crowd surrounding the blind man as Jesus notices him: "Cheer up! On your feet! He's calling you." They know hope is coming, and they tell him to get ready to meet it. It is a literal rising, in the light of being seen by Jesus—which is as much a moment to be celebrated as receiving the ability to see. It is such a beautiful gift to be visible, and the story reminds us that we are seen in our suffering and that we can be the seers of others. May you find the rise in that truth today.

35) Words with Enemies

It was just before the Passover Festival. Jesus knew that the hour had come for him to leave this world and go to the Father. Having loved his own who were in the world, he loved them to the end.

The evening meal was in progress, and the devil had

already prompted Judas, the son of Simon Iscariot,
to betray Jesus.

—John 13:1–2

The saying goes, "Keep your friends close and your enemies closer." That's always sounded counterintuitive and, frankly, pretty painful to me. I'm rarely in a hurry to have proximity with anyone who's injured me. In fact, I usually try to get some distance between myself and those people—in the name of self-preservation, peace and quiet, or just the assurance that I'm right and they're wrong. I imagine you do, too. Most of us have a growing list of former meal companions we now refuse to share a table with because of a political or theological divide or because of a wound sustained. The older I get the more disconnections I've made with people, and there's usually a story I tell myself about them in which I'm justified. Most of the time I can make a pretty strong case for excluding them. Then Jesus offers a dissenting example by setting a different table: one big enough for my enemies and for the friends who've acted like enemies.

Jesus is dining with Judas. He is serving him. Jesus knows Judas has promised to betray him, and yet there's Judas at the intimate table when Jesus shows them what it looks like to live with a servant's heart. Every once in a while, I think about that and it bothers me. It bothers me because when someone has hurt me, I'd much rather delete them from the guest list than extend hospitality to them. I'd almost always prefer to fill that empty chair with my self-righteousness and my grudges. It bothers me because I see Jesus demonstrating a love that overcomes, and I don't like to be reminded that I should at least make an attempt.

I'm not telling you to plan a meal for or to wash the feet of someone who is actively causing you pain. Without question, if you are a survivor of abuse or trauma, never place yourself in harm's way in the name of tolerating difference or loving your enemies. But within the boundaries of healthy relationships and personal safety, imagine what it might look like to rise to meet a moment of relational fracture with something other than silence and distance.

36) The Better Yes

Now Mary stood outside the tomb crying. As she wept, she bent over to look into the tomb and saw two angels in white, seated where Jesus' body had been, one at the head and the other at the foot.

They asked her, "Woman, why are you crying?"

"They have taken my Lord away," she said, "and I don't know where they have put him." At this, she turned around and saw Jesus standing there, but she did not realize that it was Jesus.

He asked her, "Woman, why are you crying? Who is it you are looking for?"

Thinking he was the gardener, she said, "Sir, if you have carried him away, tell me where you have put him, and I will get him."

Jesus said to her, "Mary."

She turned toward him and cried out in Aramaic, "Rabboni!" (which means "Teacher").

Jesus said, "Do not hold on to me, for I have not yet ascended to the Father. Go instead to my brothers and tell them, 'I am ascending to my Father and your Father, to my God and your God.'"

Mary Magdalene went to the disciples with the news: "I have seen the Lord!" And she told them that he had said these things to her.

—John 20:11–18

Today, I had a busy afternoon planned. I was running out the door to grab a workout, run some errands, and head to a writing session. As I passed my fifteen-year-old's bedroom door, he popped out and said, "Wanna go grab lunch?" "Sure thing," I said, almost involuntarily. I kind of surprised myself. On other days I might have missed that moment, but today I didn't. It was an ordinary meal, but it was also completely special and unprecedented and unrepeatable. It was the only *this day* that we would get together having *this lunch*, and I was grateful that I didn't miss it. The other things I thought I'd be doing weren't as good as this.

The last couple of chapters of John's gospel provide several scenes in which Jesus appears to his disciples following his death, but they do not recognize him. Many wiser theologians than me have ideas about the spiritual significance of it all, but I simply find the idea comforting: followers of Jesus not seeing the divinity right in front of them. I understand what it is to be oblivious to blessings or unaware of invitation. I think I most often miss Jesus because I miss people—because I am too busy or distracted to be truly present in every day that I am surrounded by human beings whose lives he said that he inhabits: the least of these, my neighbors, my loved ones, my son. Maybe being spiritual is being present and aware.

Today, the most faith-affirming thing may be to say no to something, so that you can say yes to something better, something that makes you realize Jesus is in your midst, in the next room, across the table.

37) Curb Appeal

Jesus sat down opposite the place where the offerings were put and watched the crowd putting their money into the temple treasury. Many rich people threw in large amounts. But a poor widow came and put in two very small copper coins, worth only a few cents.

Calling his disciples to him, Jesus said, "Truly I tell you, this poor widow has put more into the treasury than all the others. They all gave out of their wealth; but she, out of her poverty, put in everything—all she had to live on."

I have a confession to make, and it's nothing I'm terribly proud of: I have lawn envy. On many occasions I have actively and passionately coveted my neighbor's shrubs. It's shallow and it's ridiculous and it's counter to everything I know to be important. Still, I regularly find myself spending hours slaving over my grass and hedges and edges as if fighting for my very existence—when really, I just want to impress people next door or those driving by who I'll probably never meet, let alone know. You might be "amen"-ing right now in solidarity, recognizing your own turf-related obsessions. However, if you're silently judging me with disdain, tread carefully. Let he or she who is without jealousy cast the first eyeroll.

—MARK 12:41–44

The truth is, we all suffer from comparison sickness, even if our specific symptoms manifest themselves differently. Some of us lament how poorly our lawns appear next to other people's, or our marriages or children or careers, or our waistlines, hairlines, or bottom lines—even how spiritual we think we are when juxtaposed with other people. It is so ingrained in us to measure our lives at extremely close proximity based on what we see of others' lives from a great distance. And we're never going to measure up because their cracks and flaws are never going to be as visible as our own.

Some days it's helpful just to pause and ask the question, Why do I care about someone else's _____? (Insert whatever you use to determine your success or worth.) Picture yourself asking Jesus that question and try to imagine his response. I bet he'd tell you that you aren't in a competition here with anyone; that your life is not about how your yard or your family or your achievements look to anyone else. Today, rest in how green the grass is on this side.

38) Tough Love

"You have heard that it was said, 'Love your neighbor and hate your enemy.' But I tell you, love your enemies and pray for those who persecute you, that you may be children of your Father in heaven. He causes his sun to rise on the evil and the good, and sends rain on the righteous and the unrighteous. If you love those who love you, what reward will you get? Are not even the tax collectors doing that? And if you greet only your own people, what are you doing more than others? Do not even pagans do that? Be perfect, therefore, as your heavenly Father is perfect."

—MATTHEW 5:43–48

Today, I realized something about myself that makes me a bit sick to my stomach: I may not be all that interested in loving my enemies after all. For a long time, it was one of my go-to, sure-fire, sanctified mic drops whenever I encountered hateful people who also claimed faith. I'd lecture them that their refusal to show kindness and decency to someone (even someone they vehemently disagreed with) was disobedience to Jesus. I'd remind them that Christians are primarily defined by the way they treat those they believe to be their adversaries.

But things are different now. Now, the idea doesn't sit well with me. Suddenly, enemy-love is far more distasteful and much less mandatory. Suddenly, it's up for negotiation. It was a lot easier to aspire to loving my enemies when they didn't seem so close and so loud and so prevalent; when I didn't have so many daily reminders of just how much *loving* I'm now required to do.

I now have to love my enemy

across the table at family gatherings,
on a longtime friend's social media profile,
in my neighbor's driveway,
in the next cubicle at work,
at my son's football practice,
at the gym when he interrupts my workout
with unsolicited opinions,
at restaurants when I overhear a conversation
in the booth next to me,
driving in front of me on the highway.

When I see some of the things these people are saying and the hatred they're perpetuating and the damage they're inflicting—I'm not that interested in loving them. In fact, withholding love right now seems to be the right message to send them, to let them know how displeased I am by them. Loving them would actually be condoning their behavior, and so hating them feels almost virtuous, almost righteous. I can almost convince myself that Jesus is okay with this, that my mistreatment of my adversaries is something he blesses—that it *is* my being a good and faithful Christian.

But then, Jesus...

Today, may you love when it's toughest to love.

39) Local Weather Forecast

That day when evening came, he said to his disciples, "Let us go over to the other side." Leaving the crowd behind, they took him along, just as he was, in the boat. There were also other boats with him. A furious squall came up, and the waves broke over the boat, so that it was nearly swamped. Jesus was in the stern, sleeping on a cushion. The disciples woke him and said to him, "Teacher, don't you care if we drown?"

He got up, rebuked the wind and said to the waves, "Quiet! Be still!" Then the wind died down and it was completely calm.

He said to his disciples, "Why are you so afraid? Do you still have no faith?"

They were terrified and asked each other, "Who is this? Even the wind and the waves obey him!"

—MARK 4:35–41

A couple of years ago I was on a plane headed to a speaking event. I texted my host to let her know the that plane was about to take off, and (knowing my aversion to flying) she replied with what she *thought* were words of encouragement, words someone has probably said or written to you, or that you yourself have offered in similar situations: "OK," she wrote, "be safe." I smiled and replied, "I'll just be sitting here. You tell that to that pilot and the weather!" I wasn't really kidding. The pilot and the weather were outside of my control, and it was easy to believe that my fear (or my peace) rested in those external things outside of my control.

Difficult times tend to make us feel as if we have no control, and that lack of control is fairly terrifying. Mark describes the disciples' literally experiencing a flood of fear. The storm comes, and as happens in our lives, panic accompanies it. They are overwhelmed by the wind and the waves, even though they have Jesus as their traveling companion, even though they know his heart and have witnessed his power. They allow their outer circumstances to dictate their internal condition. They allow what they see to make them forget what they know. The disciples freak out in the middle of the chaos. They look for Jesus to bail them out, and they find him in the back of the boat power napping. He isn't sleeping because he doesn't care (something they suggest after waking him), but because his peace is not defined by anything around him.

This is our choice every single day. Though we can't affect the *pilot* or the *weather,* we do have some control in the chaos. We do have control over our response to it. We can alter our inner weather. Today, trust in the character of God and don't allow what you can see to make you forget what you know. Rest in the journey.

40) Clarity and Cloudiness

"Enter through the narrow gate. For wide is the gate
and broad is the road that leads to destruction, and
many enter through it. But small is the gate and
narrow the road that leads to life, and only a few
find it."

—Matthew 7:13–14

Sometimes I wish Jesus wasn't so clear: such as when he's telling me that I need to love my enemies, or that I have to forgive people as many times as they ask me to, or that I can't worship God and money simultaneously. In those moments, his clarity is uncomfortable and inconvenient—and, frankly, annoying because it stretches me where I'd rather not be stretched, and lovingly but forcefully nudges me from behavior that I've gotten used to. So often in my life, I've encountered the bluntness and matter-of-factness of Jesus and looked for a loophole that would exempt me from what seemed obvious, or tried to find an alternative interpretation of scripture that didn't necessitate my being as loving or forgiving or generous as it appears he wants me to be.

Other times though, I really wish Jesus had spoken with far greater clarity: for example, when he tells Martha that her sister Mary has chosen the "one thing" that is needed but doesn't explicitly name what that one thing is, or when he instructs us to "store up treasures in heaven" but neglects to describe specifically how such transactions are initiated. Or in this passage, where he talks about a narrow road leading to life that few find. I've read or heard that verse preached hundreds of times, and yet precisely cracking the code has never been all that simple. I want to be among those minority narrow-roaders, but locating it often feels nebulous and elusive. Yet maybe the mystery isn't all that mysterious. Maybe if I live attentively to the clear words, maybe if I stretch where they stretch me and allow myself to be nudged when they nudge me, then the narrow road will end up being the place my feet are already.

Today, receive the clarity and the mystery with equal joy.

41) The Choice in Suffering

They went to a place called Gethsemane, and Jesus said to his disciples, "Sit here while I pray." He took Peter, James and John along with him, and he began to be deeply distressed and troubled. "My soul is overwhelmed with sorrow to the point of death," he said to them. "Stay here and keep watch."

Going a little farther, he fell to the ground and prayed that if possible the hour might pass from him. "Abba, Father," he said, "everything is possible for you. Take this cup from me. Yet not what I will, but what you will."

—MARK 14:32–36

I've never had a tremendous amount of peace with the phrase, *Everything happens for a reason.* I think it gives the terrible stuff too much power, too much poetry—as if there *must* be nobility and purpose within the brutal devastation that we may find ourselves sitting in. In our profound distress, this idea forces us to run down dark, twisted rabbit trails, looking for the specific part of "The Greater Plan" that this suffering all fits into. We stutter and stop to try and find the *why's* of all of the suffering, instead of just admitting that maybe there is no *why* to be found and that perhaps this all simply sucks on a grand scale.

It's exhausting enough to endure the dark hours here and not lose our religion, without the addition of a Maker who also makes us bleed. Instead, I prefer to understand God as One who bleeds along with us: who sits with us in our agony and weeps, not causing us our distress but providing a steady, holy presence in it. In this way, I believe in suffering as a sacred space, one where we get to choose.

As much as I hate to admit it, my times of deepest anguish have almost always been the catalyst for my greatest learning, but I could have easily learned different lessons had I chosen differently. Yes, I grew tremendously in those trying times, but I could have grown in another direction altogether with another choice. In that way, those moments of devastation held no single, microscopic, needle-in-the-haystack truth to hunt for while I grieved and struggled, but there was still treasure to be found in the making of my choices and in their ripples. No, I don't believe that everything happens for a reason, but I do believe there is *meaning* in how we respond to all things that happen to us, even when they are not at all good things.

Today, be encouraged as you suffer and choose.

42) Hard Religion

Thomas said to him, "My Lord and my God!"

Then Jesus told him, "Because you have seen me, you have believed; blessed are those who have not seen and yet have believed."

—JOHN 20:28–29

Every day I meet people in free fall. They come to me in the middle of nagging questions or full-on existential crises. Due to a tragedy they've experienced, or a disturbing reality about the world they're now fully reckoning with, or simply a conflict in their minds that they can't think or pray themselves out of, they're questioning something, perhaps everything. These are parents, doctors, restaurant workers, police officers, Christian influencers, and, yes, even ministers. And most of the time, they show up in my inbox or to a speaking event or at a church—not only with their questions, but with the guilt that they have the questions at all. That's because many of us who have been raised in a religious tradition have also been raised to see certainty as a virtue, to believe that questions point to a deficiency in our character or a moral failing. I always remind people that if God is God, God knows exactly the reasons you believe what you believe and the reasons you struggle to believe what you can no longer believe. And God is OK with that.

After Jesus allows Thomas what he needs to touch and to see in order to believe, he essentially says to Thomas, "You have the luxury of having me right here in front of you in real time and so you've come around, but most people will not. Kudos to them for what they are able to believe." With two thousand years between us and these stories, it can be a daily battle to hold on to our beliefs, to claim them as true, especially with so much in front of us that threatens to shake us from that assurance. Faith is not easy. Anyone who tells you that it is, is either intentionally or subconsciously misleading themselves or you, or perhaps both. In those moments (perhaps even in this moment) when belief is elusive and when believing feels like work, don't compound it all by feeling badly about it. Jesus has been rooting for you since he was here.

43) Woe Is Me

When Jesus had finished speaking, a Pharisee invited him to eat with him; so he went in and reclined at the table. But the Pharisee was surprised when he noticed that Jesus did not first wash before the meal.

Then the Lord said to him, "Now then, you Pharisees clean the outside of the cup and dish, but inside you are full of greed and wickedness. You foolish people! Did not the one who made the outside make the inside also? But now as for what is inside you—be generous to the poor, and everything will be clean for you."

— Luke 11:37–41

I love this passage a lot more than I should. Jesus is sharing a meal with a group of rather self-righteous believers, when in a brazenly passive-aggressive move, one of them feigns outrage at his disregard for their traditional ceremonial displays of piety. *Bad idea.* Jesus confronts them on their hypocrisy and their showy faith, and for the next few paragraphs proceeds to completely dismantle their motives and their methods, scolding them for pretending to be something they aren't, for losing the plot and missing the point, for perverting their tradition. Every time I read the passage, I cheer a little inside because I like the idea of arrogant religious people getting their comeuppance. I picture them squirming in their seats (despite the fact that they're actually reclining on the floor) and imagine their jaws dropping as they face accountability from a Jesus who refuses to let them off easy. It feels good to put myself into that scene—until I realize that I might not get out unscathed. In fact, I very well could be on the receiving end of a bunch of these relentless *woes* of Jesus.

One of the universal blinds spots we have is in the mirror. Even if we struggle with self-esteem and feelings of inadequacy, we're usually able to muster just enough ego to be able to look down on someone else for getting their religion more wrong than we get ours. We can easily spot the flaws and failings of other people and feel the brief emotional rush of the illusion of moral superiority. As I've adopted a more progressive spirituality, I've noticed how tempting it is to look down on people whose theology no longer matches my own, people who believe what I once believed or still reside in a headspace that I used to occupy myself. In those moments, I realize that even though I may have outgrown the doctrines and rituals, I haven't outgrown the hubris that elevates me above them. It's a dangerous kind of rise that I need to confront and oppose and reject hourly. Maybe I shouldn't rejoice in the idea of Jesus leveling fraudulent religious people. Maybe I should just rejoice in a grace that dines with them despite it all.

44) When, Jesus?

Now when Jesus saw the crowds, he went up on a mountainside and sat down. His disciples came to him, and he began to teach them.

He said:

"Blessed are the poor in spirit,
  for theirs is the kingdom of heaven.
Blessed are those who mourn,
  for they will be comforted.
Blessed are the meek,

for they will inherit the earth.
Blessed are those who hunger and thirst for
righteousness,
  for they will be filled.
Blessed are the merciful,
  for they will be shown mercy.
Blessed are the pure in heart,
  for they will see God.
Blessed are the peacemakers,
  for they will be called children of God.
Blessed are those who are persecuted because of
righteousness,
  for theirs is the kingdom of heaven.

"Blessed are you when people insult you, persecute
you and falsely say all kinds of evil against you
because of me."

—MATTHEW 5:1–11

A former pastor and I were having lunch a few years ago, talking about persevering in difficult times. I was struggling with a particularly painful season, and of course our conversation turned to the challenge of faith when everything seems to be falling apart. He smiled and said to me, "John, they say that God is always right on time. I believe this is true. Unfortunately, He's rarely early." He didn't need to say any more than that. I just needed someone to name and justify my impatience with things as they were and to know that someone got it.

I've always loved the Beatitudes: this opening section of the Sermon on the Mount where Jesus lists off these sacred postures or better ways of being in the world, all attached to coming blessings. The older I've gotten and the more I've paid attention to the world and to the suffering and injustices afflicting it, the more impatient I've become reading these words. I've internally responded to Jesus' declarations with a desperate one-word petition: When?

The mourning will be comforted.
When, Jesus?
The meek will inherit the earth.
When, Jesus?
The hungry will be filled.
When, Jesus?
The merciful will be shown mercy.
When, Jesus?

I know all the narrative of the Scriptures and of the story—of the eventual wiping away of tears and the alleviating of hunger and the banishing of suffering—but I confess that I wish I could see that happen more here and more now, that the blessings Jesus speaks about would be tangible and clear and present. Yet, I know many of these promises will be dreams deferred and joys postponed. It's OK to have hope and yet still feel frustrated. I think we can believe in a coming day of peace that passes all understanding, but to say in our days when that kind of peace feels impossible: When Jesus?

45) Unlovable Neighbors

"You have heard that it was said, 'Love your neighbor and hate your enemy.' But I tell you, love your enemies and pray for those who persecute you."
—MATTHEW 5:43–44

I don't like public hot tubs. They combine two things that I'm generally not fond of combining: semi-nudity and small talk with strangers. Being an introvert, I usually avoid occasions where socializing in a swimsuit is required— especially if I'm not certain just who I'll be sharing a tiny, steaming pool with—without having a solid exit strategy in place. Invariably, I find myself next to someone I'd rather have some distance from. Recently, our family was staying at a resort at the North Carolina shore where I was to officiate the wedding ceremony of a friend. The unseasonably cold temperatures and overcast skies left us surprisingly chilled after an hour or so on the beach, and as we sprinted toward our rooms to get out of the stiff winds, I spotted the oversized bathtub with three people already in it, and in a moment of uncharacteristic impulsiveness I quickly hopped in. I realized almost immediately that it was a terrible lapse in judgment.

I soon found myself seated next to the absolute *last* guy I'd have chosen to share that confined space with. I won't detail our conversation here, but suffice it to say we don't watch the same news networks, don't share a political party, and didn't vote for the same candidate in the last couple of elections. I'd like to say that after being partially submerged next to this man, the wonderfully pulsating, near-scalding water allowed us to relax and to find common ground and to realize how alike we really were—but that didn't happen. Honestly, I found him insufferable and rude and hateful, and I didn't do anything to hide that fact until finally getting up and walking away.

Hours later I thought about the man. He has a story. and I wasn't interested in it. I justified my coldness with him. Yet, if I believe this faith thing, then I believe God made him, too. I believe that his story is important. For a few minutes he was my noisy and intrusive neighbor, and I didn't find much love for him. And what Jesus tells me is that this is a *me* problem. The call to love our neighbors doesn't come with the caveat that they need to first make themselves more lovable. I don't get to choose who I show decency toward. In this life, we don't get to make our enemies more lovable; we get to be a little kinder while we're sitting here together.

46) Afraid and Joyful

After the Sabbath, at dawn on the first day of the week, Mary Magdalene and the other Mary went to look at the tomb.

There was a violent earthquake, for an angel of the Lord came down from heaven and, going to the tomb, rolled back the stone and sat on it. His appearance was like lightning, and his clothes were white as snow. The guards were so afraid of him that they shook and became like dead men.

The angel said to the women, "Do not be afraid, for I know that you are looking for Jesus, who was crucified. He is not here; he has risen, just as he said. Come and see the place where he lay. Then go quickly and tell his disciples: 'He has risen from the dead and is going ahead of you into Galilee. There you will see him.' Now I have told you."

So the women hurried away from the tomb, afraid yet filled with joy, and ran to tell his disciples. Suddenly Jesus met them. "Greetings," he said. They came to him, clasped his feet and worshiped him. Then Jesus said to them, "Do not be afraid. Go and tell my brothers to go to Galilee; there they will see me."

—MATTHEW 28:1–10

"I guess you had to be there." We've all spoken those words when we could not make someone understand the power or the joy or the depth of a moment.

We need to end where we began: at the site of the unthinkable, at the epicenter of hope's restoration, at the specific geographic spot where the *rise of all rises* is documented. Matthew records this occasion when love really has the last, loudest word and the word is getting out. I don't know whether you read this passage and you receive the story at face value—or whether you find in the words a metaphor for your own rise from the valleys and the tombs and the lost causes you've experienced. Either way, resurrections give us a testimony that no one else is capable of and that we have trouble explaining. They let us tell people what we've seen and what we know and how beyond belief it all is.

In this final day together, I want to call your attention to Matthew's description of the women as they leave the tomb, after having just witnessed the firsthand presence of Jesus: *afraid yet filled with joy*. That is this honest spiritual journey, that place of paradox and tension. I recognize the condition well, and I imagine you do, too. It is triumph even with the mystery surrounding it; it is the front-row seat to something your eyes can hardly believe, the excitement to run and tell people a story you can't quite fathom yourself. I picture these women sprinting breathlessly to give Jesus' shattered students the news that they know will demolish the sadness they'd started to get used to. I see a combustible moment within and among the disciples, a time when everything else was worth it: all the fear, the sacrifice, the doubts, the praying, the waiting. I imagine their spirits rising stratospherically and nothing ever being the same again. I bet they were afraid and filled with joy, too.

The rise is something we don't get until we do. We don't receive it until we fall. It does not come until the sadness first arrives. We don't have that moment of awe and gratitude until after some extended time in the valley or the darkness or the grieving. Sometimes we simply endure the night and allow the morning to surprise us with news that changes us. May the dawn be coming just on the horizon. May your rise be on the way.